A HANDBOOK OF ETIQUETTE
FOR YOUNG LADIES
AND GENTLEMEN
TO BE USED AS A GUIDE
FOR EVERYDAY
SOCIAL BEHAVIOR

BY *Sesyle Joslin*. PICTURES BY *Maurice Sendak*

HarperCollins*Publishers*

What
Do
You
Say,
Dear?

You are downtown and there is a gentleman giving baby elephants to people. You want to take one home because you have always wanted a baby elephant, but first the gentleman introduces you to each other.

What do you say, dear?

How do you do?

You are picking dandelions and columbines outside the castle. Suddenly a fierce dragon appears and blows red smoke at you, but just then a brave knight gallops up and cuts off the dragon's head.

What do you say, dear?

Thank you very much.

You are a cowboy riding around the range. Suddenly Bad-Nose Bill comes up behind you with a gun. He says, "Would you like me to shoot a hole in your head?"

What do you say, dear?

No, thank you.

You are a nurse and you rush to see a
patient because a dinosaur bit him.
You bandage him all up, and he says, "Oh,
Nurse, you have saved my life. Thank you."

What do you say, dear?

You're welcome.

You have gone downtown to do some shopping.
You are walking backwards, because sometimes
you like to, and you bump into a crocodile.

What do you say, dear?

Excuse me.

You are at a wedding party because you are the bride. You have a fine husband and an enormous wedding cake and you are going to live happily ever after, only first you are very, very hungry.

What do you say, dear?

Would you please pass the cake?

You are at the Princess' ball, and she is telling you a secret, but her orchestra of bears is making such a fearful lot of noise you cannot hear what she is saying.

What do you say, dear?

I beg your pardon.

You go to London to see the Queen. She says, "Oh, you must stay for dinner. We are having spaghetti." So you do, and there is spaghetti for the appetizer, spaghetti for the main dish, and a spaghetti salad. By the time the Queen's guard brings spaghetti for dessert, you cannot fit in your chair any more and you want to leave the table.

What do you say, dear?

May I please be excused?

You are flying around in your airplane and
you remember that the Duchess said, "Do
drop in for tea sometime."
So you do, only it makes a rather large hole
in her roof.

What do you say, dear?

I'm sorry.

You are a dangerous pirate and you have captured a fine lady to take on your ship. Every morning when you untie her so she can eat breakfast, she says, "Good morning. How are you?"

What do you say, dear?

Fine, thank you. How are you?

All your friends come to your house for a
party. The Princess brings her orchestra
of bears and they play two dances, but then
they want to eat everybody up.

What do you say, dear?

This is the end. Goodbye.

First published by
Addison-Wesley Publishing Company
Copyright © 1958 by Sesyle Joslin
Copyright © renewed 1986 by Sesyle Joslin
Printed in the U.S.A. All rights reserved
Library of Congress Catalog Card Number 84–43140
ISBN 0-201-09391-X
ISBN 0-06-023074-6 (lib. bdg.)

THIS WAS FOR

Victoria, Alexandra, Julia, and

Awich Hine Buff